Garden Spiders

Live in My Backyard

Text and Photos by Nannette Richford

ISBN-13:978-1539465881
ISBN-10:1539465888

Colorful Garden Spiders

The female *Black and Yellow Garden Spider* (Argiope aurantia) is one of the biggest spiders you will find in your backyard. Her head and body can grow to more than an inch long, but her long, slender legs make her look much bigger.

This spider has a furry gray head and a black abdomen with bright-yellow markings. It has eight legs and eight eyes.

The male *Black and Yellow Garden Spider* is much smaller than the female and does not have the bright markings.

How can you tell this is a female black and yellow garden spider?

In the Garden and Along Roadsides

The *Black and Yellow Garden Spider* lives in gardens and along roadsides. You may find her in the flower bed or in the tall grass near the garden.

During the spring and early summer, she is hard to see because she is still small. By late summer and early fall, she has grown to full-size and is easier to see.

She usually builds a web in one spot and stays in the same place for weeks. Sometimes, she will move her web if she is disturbed or if she cannot catch enough food.

Do you think this garden spider will find enough food in my garden?

Why Do They Make Webs?

The *Black and Yellow Garden Spider* is an orb weaver spider. That means she spins a web that is round or shaped like an orb.

It looks like a big wagon wheel with a hub in the middle and spokes leading to the outside of the web.

Her web is usually about two feet wide. It is often hidden in the grass where she can catch flies and bugs that visit the flowers.

When the bugs land it the web, they get stuck and cannot fly or crawl away.

Can you see the spokes in this web?

How Does She Make the Web?

The *Black and Yellow Garden Spider* begins spinning her web by making silk in her spinnerets. The spinnerets are located on the underside of her abdomen.

The silk floats in the wind until it touches a plant stem or other object. The silk sticks to the stems of the plants. The spider then makes the spokes of the web.

Next, she connects the spokes to make concentric circles to fill the web. The concentric circles start out small in the center, called the hub, and get bigger as they reach toward the outside of the web.

Can you find the silk coming out of this garden spider's spinnerets?

What's That Writing in the Web?

The *Black and Yellow Garden Spider* is sometimes called a writing spider because she makes a zig-zagged structure, called a stabilimenta, in her web. Some people think the stabilimenta looks like handwriting. It is made from silk and is usually found near the center of the spider's web

Scientists do not know for sure why garden spiders make a stabilimenta. Some scientists think it stops birds from flying into the web. Others think it makes the web stronger. Maybe she is sending a secret message.

Why do you think the Black and Yellow Garden Spider makes a stabilimenta?

Just Hanging Out

After she builds her web, the *Black and Yellow Garden Spider* hangs in the center of the web and waits to catch bugs and flying insects.

She holds her legs spread out in pairs so that it looks like she only has four legs.

She hangs upside down with her gray, furry head pointing downward and her abdomen pointing upward.

Can you find all eight legs on this garden spider?

Dinner Time

When insects fly or crawl too close to the web they get stuck on the sticky silk. The garden spider rushes to the insect and grabs it with her claws.

She uses her pedipalps, two tiny leg-like growths, to help hold the prey. This garden spider has furry, gray pedipalps.

First she bites the insect to kill it. Next, she wraps it in silk to save it for a tasty meal later.

Sometimes she will wrap up several insects to save for later.

Can you find the spider's pedipalps?

Rebuilding the Web

At night, the *Black and Yellow Garden Spider* rebuilds or repairs her web. She eats the old silk. She uses the old silk to make new silk to repair the web.

She spins new silk and attaches it to the spokes, using her legs and tiny claws to hold the silk in place.

If her whole web is damaged, she may eat the entire web and build another one in the same place. Most of the time she repairs or rebuilds small parts of the web that have been damaged.

How many of this spider's legs are holding onto the web?

Making an Egg Sac

In the late summer, the *Black and Yellow Garden Spider* makes an egg sac to hold her eggs. She lays hundreds of tiny eggs in the sac and hangs it near her web.

The egg sac is teardrop shaped and is brown or golden. It looks like brown paper.

The egg sac is camouflaged so it is difficult to see in the grass and leaves when they turn brown in the fall.

Why do you think the egg sac is camouflaged?

Making a Web Around the Egg Sac

After making and hanging the egg sac, the *Black and Yellow Garden Spider* spends all day spinning a tangled web around the egg sac.

This tangled web protects the egg sac from birds and insects and gives the baby spiders a place to hatch and grow.

The egg sac keeps the eggs safe and dry. It will hang in the same place all winter.

Can you see the tangled web around the egg sac?

Protecting the Egg Sac

By the end of the day, the egg sac and the tangled web are finished. The mother spider hangs upside down in the web near the egg sac to rest and protect the eggs.

She will guard the egg sac until the first frost in the fall, but she will not live to see her babies.

The mother *Black and Yellow Garden Spider* will die when the weather gets too cold.

What do you think will happen to the eggs when the mother dies?

Spiderlings Come Out in the Spring

The eggs inside the egg sac hatch in the fall. But the baby spiders, called spiderlings, don't crawl out of the sac yet. They wait until the warm weather returns in the spring.

In the spring, hundreds of tiny *Black and Yellow Garden Spiders* will crawl out of the egg sac. They are so small that they look like specks of dust.

Can you see the tiny spiderlings?

Getting Ready to Leave Home

Before they get ready to find their own home, the spiderlings live together in a cluster on a stem.

When they are ready to leave, the spiderlings let out a strand of silk that catches in the wind and carries them to their new homes. This is called ballooning. The tiny thread of silk is called gossamer.

The spiderlings grow quickly and soon make webs of their own.

By late summer or early fall, the new spiders will build an egg sac and lay eggs to start their life cycle all over again.

Would you like to see a cluster of spiderlings?

Vocabulary

Ballooning: Letting out a thin thread of silk that catches in the wind to move spiderlings to a new area.

Camouflage: To hide, usually with colors that blend in with the surroundings.

Cluster: A group of things crowded closely together.

Concentric Rings: Rings or circles that have the same center.

Dormant: A state when the spiders do not grow.

Gossamer: The thin threads of silk used in ballooning.

Orb: Round or shaped like a circle.

Pedipalps: Tiny leg-like structures used to hold prey.

Spiderlings: Baby spiders

Spinnerets: The organs on the spider's abdomen that make silk.

Stabilimenta: Zig zagged marking in the spider web that look like writing.

Strand: A thin string.

Spider Facts

• Spiders are not insects. They are arachnids.

• Spiders have eight legs and two body parts, but insects have six legs and three body parts.

• Most spiders have eight eyes, but some spiders have more.

• Spiders do not have antennae like insects do.

• Spider's legs are covered with hair.

• Spiders have two or more tiny claws at the end of their legs.

• Spiders use the hair on their legs to sense vibrations and to smell the air.

• Spiders have oil on their body to keep them from sticking to the sticky web.

Garden Spider Craft for Kids

1. Trace the shape of the garden spider onto heavy stock paper.
Allow children to color the black and yellow design on the spider with
markers or crayons. Make legs from strips of black paper with an accordion
fold or use black pipe cleaners. Tape or staple the legs to the spider.
Set the spiders aside.

2. Paint a paper plate black and allow it to dry. Cut out the center leaving a
1-inch rim. Use a paper punch to punch holes evenly spaced around the
inside rim of the plate. Tie black yarn to one of the holes and show children
how to lace the yarn in a crisscross fashion to create a spider web.
Keep the pieces of yarn short for little hands and tie on another piece of
 yarn if the web needs more "silk".

3. Attach the spider to the center of the web with the head pointing
downward.

4. Create a garden scene bulletin board with brightly colored flowers
and plenty of tall grass.

5. Display the garden spiders on the bulletin board. You can also display the
webs hanging from the ceiling or suspended in a window.

Nannette Richford was born and raised in rural Maine. She has always been inspired by nature and has recently taken up photography to share that passion with others. As a freelance writer and photographer, she has been published on a variety of sites online.

As a mother and a former teacher, Nannette enjoys introducing children to the wonders of the world around them. Her first children's book, *Who Lives in My Backyard?* Was released in September 2016.

Black and Yellow Garden Spiders Live in My Backyard is the second book in her *In My Backyard* series. Watch for more books in this series coming soon.

www.ingramcontent.com/pod-product-compliance
Lightning Source LLC
Chambersburg PA
CBHW041535280526
45792CB00004B/1511